THE PONY EXPRESS

👆 This painting, originally titled "San Francisco Welcomes the Pony Express," illustrates the excitement of Californians at the establishment of a cross-country mail system. Though it was short-lived, the Pony Express created a stronger link between the East and West coasts.

THE PONY EXPRESS

JOHN RIDDLE

MASON CREST PUBLISHERS

Mason Crest Publishers
370 Reed Road
Broomall PA 19008
www.masoncrest.com

First printing

1 3 5 7 9 8 6 4 2

Library of Congress Cataloging-in-Publication Data
on file at the Library of Congress

ISBN 1-59084-061-5

Publisher's note: many of the quotations in this book come from
original sources, and contain the spelling and grammatical
inconsistencies of the original text.

CONTENTS

A Pony Express rider greets the station worker as he approaches. The distance between St. Joseph, Missouri, and San Francisco, California, was covered in 9 to 10 days—much faster than the six months it took mail to reach California by ship.

ON YOUR MARK, GET SET, GO!

ON APRIL 3, 1860, PEOPLE IN TWO CITIES WERE GATHERING TO WITNESS AN HISTORIC EVENT: THE birth of the Pony Express.

Shortly before noon in San Francisco, California, and the middle of the afternoon in St. Joseph, Missouri, crowds began to gather. They wanted to see the first Pony Express riders depart each city and begin the 10-day journey that would allow mail to travel between the East and the West.

The crowds were excited. After all, they were going to be part of history in the making, and they wanted a firsthand, up close look at the action. The crowds listened to many speeches that were made by government officials. But as the day wore on, people in St. Joseph were getting restless and wondered when the first rider would depart. At 6 P.M., a whole hour after the rider was scheduled to leave, officials brought out the horse that was supposed to carry the first rider. The officials wanted the crowd to be happy. They thought the people would calm down if they looked at the horse.

The horse and its equipment drew cheers from the people. The crowd looked over the sleek, streamlined saddle

Johnny Fry

The first rider to leave from St. Joseph, Missouri, on April 3, 1860, was born in 1840 in Kentucky. (Some records show his name being spelled "Frey" or "Frye.") Shortly after his birth, his family moved to Missouri, and he was little more than a boy when he began working for the Pony Express.

Legend has it that he was something of a ladies' man, even as a young teenager. Some stories have been told about how young ladies would watch for him to make his Pony Express run, and when he passed by their houses, they would hand him goodies and treats to eat. He was an avid horseback rider, and because of his skills he was able to cover his Pony Express route in record time. (His route took him from St. Joseph, Missouri, to Senaca, Kansas, a distance of 80 miles.)

When the Civil War began, he enlisted in the Union Army and was killed in action on October 6, 1863, in Baxter Springs, Kansas.

and the leather mail pouch, better known as a mochila. The people began to get so caught up in the excitement, they began pulling hair out of the bay mare.

A short time later, the first Pony Express rider came out to see the crowd of people. Johnny Fry, a Kansas ranch boy who had won many horse races, stood before the crowd and waved. He also was anxious to get started, and finally at about 7 P.M. that evening, he was able to begin the first leg of his journey.

👆 Johnny Fry was the first rider to leave St. Joseph, on April 3, 1860. Most of the Pony Express riders were young men with small frames.

The leather mail pouch known as a *mochila* was designed and made by Israel Landis of the Wyeth Company.

At the sound of the cannon, Johnny Fry galloped out of town as the crowd cheered him on. He traveled past Jules Street, and within minutes he was boarding a ferryboat that would take him and his precious cargo across the Missouri River.

After approximately 30 minutes on the ferryboat, Fry and his horse landed in Elwood, Kansas, and to begin the trip westward. The first leg of the historic journey took Fry along the Oregon Trail, a wide strip of land with little or no grass. Nearly 45 minutes after leaving Elwood, Fry arrived in the town of Troy, Kansas, to pick up a fresh horse. It took less than three minutes to switch mounts and secure the mochila.

Fry continued his swift journey, making good time along his route. He changed horses two more times, in the towns of Kennekuk and Kickapoo. Finally, at about 11:30 that night, he

The first Pony Express delivery included 49 letters, five private telegrams, and many telegraphic dispatches. It also included some copies of Eastern newspapers that had been printed on tissue, just for this occasion. The total mail weighed a little less than 15 pounds.

reached the small settlement of Granada and turned over the mochila to the next Pony Express rider.

At about 5:30 P.M. on April 13, the mail reached the town of Sacramento, California. It had taken only 10 days to complete the journey, and people everywhere were singing the praises of the Pony Express.

But could the Pony Express live up to everyone's expectations?

👆 Riders for the Pony Express scheduled only a few minutes to switch horses at the station. It usually took only moments to change the mochila—a leather mail sack—and board another horse, which was saddled and waiting for the rider's arrival.

2
AN IDEA BECOMES A REALITY

Benton Clark 1960

DURING THE FIRST HALF OF THE 19TH CENTURY, WAGON TRAINS BEGAN TAKING PEOPLE ALONG the Santa Fe Trail and Oregon Trail into the newly acquired territories of Louisiana, Oregon, and California. Getting there was not an easy journey for those brave people who made the trip. Many people were killed by Indian **ambushes** and had to deal with hunger, disease, and all types of weather.

But after gold was discovered in California in 1848, the numbers of people heading out West greatly increased. During that same year, the Post Office Department awarded a contract to the Pacific Mail Steamship Company to carry mail to California. Mail was taken by ship from New York to Panama, then moved across Panama by **rail**, and then to San Francisco by ship. The post office said it would take between three and four weeks to deliver a letter from the East to the West. However, it usually took longer.

Once the mail did arrive in San Francisco, it was piled up in a post office until a miner took the time to come in from the camps and sort through the letters looking for mail addressed to him or his friends.

Gold Rush Mail Delivery

During the California Gold Rush, several men made their fortunes not by finding shiny nuggets of gold, but by delivering the mail. One of them was Alexander Todd. He had been a clerk before moving west hoping to find gold. Once in California, however, Todd found that he was not healthy enough to spend hours panning for gold in chilly rivers.

Todd hoped to capitalize on the miners' frustration with the confusing mail situation in San Francisco. In 1849 he started a service to deliver mail between San Francisco and the nearby mining camps. For $2.50, he would carry a letter to San Francisco; from there, the letter could be posted to any town. For an ounce of gold dust, worth about $16, Todd would search through the mail in San Francisco and bring letters addressed to the miner back to his (or her) camp.

Todd signed up hundreds of miners for this service, then headed to San Francisco. There, he posted letters and searched through the piles of unsorted mail for letters addressed to his clients. This was so successful that he expanded his business, offering to take gold from the camps to banks in San Francisco. For this service he charged 5 percent of the value of the gold. Soon, Alexander Todd had become a wealthy man.

Others saw the possibilities for more efficient mail delivery in California as well. By 1853, there were at least a dozen small companies that operated stagecoach lines between the gold mines and the large cities of California.

Because of the slow mail service, people in California often received news about the rest of the country weeks after an event took place. In fact, it wasn't until after California had been admitted to the Union for a full six weeks that people in that state heard the news.

Californians were frustrated. In 1853, an article appeared in a Los Angeles newspaper about how bad the mail service was in the West. Californians wanted someone to come up with a faster way to get mail into their region.

It would be very expensive to set up a mail route that would connect the eastern and western regions of the country. For several years Californians asked for money from the United

The Oregon Trail was a pioneer route to the Pacific Northwest. It started in the vicinity of Independence, Missouri, and ended at Fort Vancouver, Washington. It was used especially between 1842 and 1860. The Santa Fe Trail was the pioneer route to the Southwest, which was used especially between 1821 and 1880. It started near Kansas City, Missouri, and ended at Santa Fe, New Mexico.

States government. In January of 1855, U.S. Senator William Gwin of California introduced a bill in the Senate that would establish a weekly mail delivery service between St. Louis and San Francisco. However, the bill never became a law. It was not until after 75,000 Californians signed a petition in 1856 that the U.S. government agreed to take action. The government promised to give a $600,000 annual mail contract to a stagecoach line, which could carry both mail and passengers on the east-west route.

👆 A station worker changes the mochila for an arriving Express rider. The workers at Pony Express stations had to be on the alert for arriving riders so they would not slow them down. Riders were expected to leave the station within two minutes; they changed horses every 10 to 15 miles.

Although the going rate for a horse at that time was around $50, the Pony Express company paid $150 to $200 for each horse. The horses were well cared for, and they were fed and housed better than some people at the time. Some riders were fond of their horses and tried their best to take care of them. However, due to conditions on the trail, sometimes a horse would fall lame and have to be destroyed. If a horse died along the trail, it usually meant that the rider had to continue on foot with the mail pouch.

The men who operated the relief stations had to be ready with a fresh horse whenever a Pony Express rider arrived. It took only about two minutes to change horses. The rider would literally leap off one horse and quickly mount another. The mochila that carried the mail had been designed to fit snugly over the horn of the saddle, so it only took a few seconds for the rider to snatch it and quickly place it on the saddle of the new horse.

The Pony Express riders and their horses were the true heroes and endured many hardships to get the mail delivered.

👆 A wheelwright works inside the Pony Express stables in St. Joseph, Missouri. These stables now house the Pony Express Museum.

THE STATIONS ALONG THE ROUTE

nearly 35,000 pieces of mail. They also traveled enough miles
to equal 24 trips around the planet earth. Along the journey,
the stations and the men who took care of everything there
played a key part in keeping the Pony Express in operation.

Between 150 and 200 stations existed in five different
divisions along the route of the Pony Express. Russell's
company was able to take advantage of the stagecoach
stations that were already established along the route that the
riders would be using. But there were not enough stations, so
new stations had to be built. In the days leading up to the
launch of the Pony Express on April 3, 1860, crews were
dispatched to build the necessary stations.

Depending upon the location of the Pony Express stations,
different materials were used to construct them. In both the
eastern and western parts of the route, the stations were built
using lumber or logs. But in western Utah and Nevada, the
stations were made out of **adobe** bricks. Sometimes those

bricks were made on the spot where the station was being built. Other times, stones were laid on top of each other without even using anything for mortar. In Nebraska, some stations were built using just sod, while in Wyoming the rough buildings were made of either logs or adobe bricks. Because time was a factor in getting all of the stations ready for the launch date of the Pony Express, some stations ended up being nothing more than a large hole in a hillside that was covered over with logs, brush, or a dirt roof.

The locations of the stations was determined strictly by the distance a horse could run while maintaining the demanding pace of 10 to 12 miles per hour. When the Pony Express first started operating, the stations were located about 25 miles apart. However, it was determined that this was too far apart, so more stations were added. When all of the stations were ready and fully operating, they ended up being between 10 and 15 miles apart.

Each of the five divisions was placed at 150- to 200-mile intervals and was run by a division superintendent. It was his job to see that the stretch of trail assigned to him ran smoothly. That meant that he had to make sure all the stations along his route had enough supplies. He also had to take care of the livestock and make sure there was enough food and water. The division superintendent hired replacement Pony Express riders if a rider quit or was injured and could no longer ride the route. The division superintendent watched for

👆 When they were not charging across the country, Pony Express horses were kept in corrals, one of which can be seen behind the rider in this Frederic Remington illustration. Horses were expensive; they were also necessary for the success of the Pony Express. Therefore, it was very important to provide good stables and care for the animals.

Indian attacks, and he was responsible for keeping away horse thieves and **cattle rustlers**.

At each of the individual station locations, a station keeper and a stock tender kept a watchful eye to see when a Pony Express rider was approaching. Their job was to make sure a fresh horse was saddled and ready to go. But even though

Frank E. Webner, a Pony Express rider, sits atop his horse in this 1861 photograph. Although the mail service only lasted 18 months, it changed the East-West relations of America forever.

there was a schedule of when to
expect the next Pony Express rider,
sometimes the riders ran late.
However, the station keeper and
stock tender still had to have a
horse mounted and ready at a
moment's notice for when the rider
finally did arrive. Because of the
tight schedule, station keepers knew
better than to keep a rider waiting.

When a Pony Express rider
arrived at a relay station, he
was supposed to switch to
a fresh horse and be on his
way within two minutes.
The riders changed horses
every 10 to 15 miles. Riders
were switched about every
75 miles.

A typical station had at least
three or four horses that had to be
kept in **corrals** that were located within a few feet of the
structure. The stock tender's job was to make sure that those
horses were fed and watered. In some locations this was not
an easy task, because grass and water were not nearby. This
meant that the stock tender had to bring water in barrels for
the horses to drink, and then drive the horses to a grassy area
to be fed.

Many of the stations along the route were simple
structures with little or no furniture. It wasn't unusual to find
a station with nothing more than a dirt floor and wooden
crates for tables and chairs. When it was time for the station
keeper and stock tender to go to bed, they had a choice of
either sleeping on the dirt floor or sacking outside on the
straw or hay.

5

DANGER ALONG THE WAY

THE PONY EXPRESS RIDERS WERE A BRAVE BUNCH OF MEN WHO RISKED their life every time they mounted and departed from a station. They never knew what was ahead of them on their journey. The weather could sometimes be so brutal that both horse and rider barely survived. The worst route of the Pony Express was along the **sierra** between Nevada and California. This stretch of the journey was approximately 85 miles long. During the wintertime, the conditions slowed riders down. And just as the cold could be brutal to the rider and his horse, the heat from the desert was just as unbearable along other stretches of the trail.

A Pony Express rider enters the station in this 19th-century newspaper drawing. On the open plains, the riders often faced danger of an attack by Indians or bandits.

Newspaper advertisements for Pony Express riders hinted at the dangers of the job. They said the company was looking for "daring young men, preferably orphans." Riders were paid $100 to $150 a month, and the company gave them food and a place to live. They had to agree not to drink or swear while on duty.

But it wasn't only the weather that brought danger to the Pony Express riders. Along the way they had to deal with outlaws, horse thieves, and **renegade** Indian attacks. During one of the most famous Indian attacks, the mail did not make it through.

In May 1860, about 6,000 Paiutes, members of an Indian tribe in Nevada, caused some big trouble for the Pony Express riders. According to newspaper accounts, the Indians had faced a long and harsh winter, in which many of them died from exposure to the cold and the elements. By the time spring rolled around, many of the Native Americans were angry and blamed all of their troubles on the white man. The entire tribe looked as if it were getting ready to declare war and attack. However, a Paiute chief named Numaga tried to keep the rest of his people calm. He told them they shouldn't attack any of the white men. He tried to convince them that the white man was not responsible for the losses they had suffered from the previous harsh winter.

He had almost all of the Paiutes under control when a few renegades broke away from the tribe and raided the Williams Station of the Pony Express. In the attack, they

The Pony Express stamp was flanked by two bears to demonstrate the unwavering determination of its riders. The cost of sending mail cross-country did not compensate for the cost of lives lost by Indian attacks.

William F. Cody

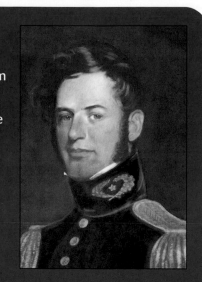

Probably one of the most well known Pony Express riders, William F. Cody was born on February 26, 1845, in Scott County, Iowa. At the young age of 15 he started working as a Pony Express rider; later he received the nickname Buffalo Bill because he was an expert buffalo hunter. As a Pony Express rider, at first he was only given a short 45-mile run along the route, but after a few months, he was transferred to a station in Wyoming, where he is said to have made the longest nonstop ride from Red Buttes Station to the Rocky Ridge Station and back when he discovered that his relief rider had been killed by Indians. He made record time and completed the journey of 322 miles over one of the most dangerous portions of the entire trail in nearly 22 hours, with 21 horses. Many stories and legends have been told about this man, and his character has come to life in movies and television. He died on January 10, 1917, in Denver, Colorado.

killed five men. The next few weeks proved to be fatal for many other Pony Express riders as the renegade Indians continued their attacks on relay stations. Before the hostilities were all over, 16 Pony Express employees were killed, and over 150 horses had been driven away from the relief stations.

The Indian attacks did not stop until the Army got involved in the fighting. By early June, the Pony Express and its riders returned to their normal operations.

The Pony Express riders also faced other dangers besides problems with foul weather and attacks from renegade Indians. Since each rider averaged 75 miles each trip, accidents were bound to occur. During his route, each rider rode between three to seven horses. With that many different horses combined with the length of trail, sometimes a horse would stumble and a rider would be thrown. When that happened, the rider was slowed down while he stopped to nurse his wounds.

In one recorded incident, a Pony Express rider by the name of William Boulton actually had to deliver the mail on foot after his horse gave out. Luckily for him, the next relief station was only five miles away, where he picked up a fresh horse and was able to continue along his scheduled route.

Another incident happened to a Pony Express rider named James W. Brink, nicknamed Dock, who was one of the earliest Pony Express riders, having been hired in April of 1860. He was a dedicated and faithful courier, but he earned his place in the history books when he and an associate fought and killed the McCandless gang of outlaws. His associate's name was Wild Bill Hickok.

Bob Haslam, who was known to everyone as Pony Bob, rode a distance of 120 miles in eight hours and 10 minutes in March 1861. He was carrying newly elected President Abraham Lincoln's inaugural address. Along the way he was ambushed by

route through the southern states.

Unfortunately, William Russell had become involved in illegal dealings. Hoping to raise money to bail out his struggling company, he and a government clerk tried to steal millions of dollars worth of government bonds. Their plan was not a success. Russell's criminal activities were discovered, and by December 1860 he was in jail, his firm financially ruined.

But it wasn't just the financial problems that caused the end of the Pony Express. On June 16, 1860, only about 10 weeks after the first Pony Express riders had departed from their respective cities on the east and west coasts, Congress passed a bill that provided money to build a transcontinental telegraph line. The line would connect the Missouri River with the Pacific Coast. Work on the telegraph line went at a breakneck pace of nearly 25 miles a day. That meant that as swiftly as the ponies were running, the telegraph poles were slowly catching up. The last gap between the poles was closed in Salt Lake City, Utah, on October 24, 1861. Five days later, the first coast-to-coast telegram was delivered. The Pony Express was no longer as needed to connect east and west.

The network of electrical lines that dotted the landscape had become the final nail in the coffin of the Pony Express. The Pony Express riders kept delivering mail via their established route all the way up until November 1861. They had served their country well. They had brought people closer

👆 Although only in service for a relatively short time, the Pony Express captured the imagination of the country. When it did eventually end, many newspapers published supportive editorials about the unique service.

While traveling in a stage coach, Mark Twain observed a Pony Express rider and wrote this observation:

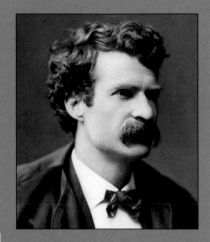

We had a consuming desire from the beginning to see a pony rider; but somehow or other all that passed us, and all that met us managed to streak by in the night and so we heard only a whiz and a hail, and the swift phantom of the desert was gone before we could get our heads out of the windows. But now we were expecting one along every moment, and would see him in broad daylight. Presently the driver exclaims: "Here he comes!"

Every neck is stretched further and every eye strained wider across the endless dead level of the prairie, a black speck appears against the sky, and it is plain that it moves. Well I should think so! In a second it comes a horse and rider, rising and falling, rising and falling—sweeping toward us nearer and nearer growing more and more distinct, more and more sharply defined—nearer and still nearer, and the flutter of hoofs comes faintly to the ear—another instant a whoop and a hurrah from our upper deck, a wave of the rider's hands but no reply and the man and horse burst past our excited faces and go winging away like the belated fragment of a storm!

So sudden is it all, and so like a flash of unreal fancy, that but for a flake of white foam left quivering and perishing on a mail sack after the vision had flashed by and disappeared, we might have doubted whether we had seen any actual horse and man at all, maybe.

together and enabled mail to be delivered between Missouri and California faster than ever before.

Some of the relay stations were torn down, while others were sold or left to fall into decay due to lack of upkeep. The remaining horses were sold, and the riders had to find new jobs. Most of them probably went on to jobs that were far less dangerous. They were left with memories that would last a lifetime, and they no doubt had plenty of stories to tell their grandchildren.

Many newspapers dedicated stories praising the service provided by the Pony Express. In an editorial the *California Pacific* wrote:

A fast and faithful friend has the Pony been to our far off state. Summer and winter, storm and shine, day and night, he has traveled like a weaver's shuttle back and forth till now his work is done. Good-bye, Pony! No proud and star-caparisoned charger in the war field has ever done so great, so true, and so good a work as thine. No pampered and world-famed racer of the turf will ever win from you the proud fame of the fleet courser of the continent. You came to use with tidings that made your feet beautiful on the tops of the mountains; tidings of the world's great life, of nations rising for liberty and winning the day of battles, and nations' defeats and reverses. We have looked to you as those who wait for the morning, and how seldom you did fail us! When days were months and hours weeks, how you thrilled us out

GLOSSARY

Adobe
Bricks made out of sun-dried mud and straw.

Ambush
An unexpected attack by a person or group of people who are hidden.

Bandit
A robber who steals from travelers, usually at gunpoint.

Cattle rustlers
Thieves who steal cattle.

Continental Divide
A massive area of high ground in the interior of a continent, from either side of which a continent's waterways and rivers flow in different directions.

Corrals
A pen or enclosure for horses or other livestock.

Ford
To cross a river or stream at a shallow place.

Hands
A unit of measure used to determine the height of a horse. A hand is equal to four inches.

Mustangs
Wild horses that lived on the American plains.

Rail
Train or railroad.

Relay stations
Regular stopping places along a route, providing riders a chance to switch to fresh horses, or to stop for food and rest.

Renegade
An individual who rejects lawful behavior.

Sierra
A mountain range.

Slouch hat
A soft, usually felt hat with a wide flexible brim.

Subsidy
A grant or gift of money from a government to a private company to help it continue to function.

Thoroughbreds
A purebred horse that is small and fast.

Transcontinental
Extending across a continent.

TIMELINE

January 24, 1848

James Marshall discovers gold at Sutter's Mill, California.

1849

The California gold rush begins, as about 90,000 gold seekers arrive in the region.

1854

The freight hauling firm of Russell, Majors & Waddell is formed in Leavenworth, Kansas.

1857

The Butterfield Overland Mail Company receives a federal contract for $600,000 a year to deliver mail from Missouri to California.

September 16, 1858

Cross-country mail service begins as Butterfield stagecoaches set out from San Francisco and Tipton, Missouri, traveling in opposite directions. Mail delivery takes about 25 days.

1859

William Russell creates a western mail stagecoach service that eventually becomes the Central Overland, California & Pike's Peak Express. It is a financial failure.

April 3, 1860

The Pony Express is officially launched. Johnny Fry becomes the first rider to depart from St. Joseph, Missouri; in San Francisco, a rider named James Randall carries the first saddlebag filled with mail headed toward the East.

April 4, 1860

Pony Express rider Sam Hamilton leaves Sacramento, California, at 2:45 A.M. to make the first eastbound run.

April 13, 1860

Pony Express rider Sam Hamilton arrives with the first eastern mail in Sacramento, California.

April 23, 1860

Pony Express rider Sam Hamilton delivers the mochila to Thomas Bedford, another rider, and the first westbound mail to be routed overland between Sacramento and Oakland arrives in Benicia, California.

May 1860

Pony Express mail is suspended during the Paiute Indian uprising.

October 18, 1861

The westward building crew of the transcontinental telegraph project arrives in Salt Lake City, Utah.

October 24, 1861

The transcontinental telegraph project is completed when the eastward building crew arrives in Salt Lake City, Utah, to connect the lines.

October 26, 1861

The Pony Express officially ceases operations.

November 21, 1861

Last run of the Pony Express is completed.

FURTHER READING

Anderson, Peter. *The Pony Express*. New York: Grolier Publishing, 1996.

Benson, Joe. *The Traveler's Guide to the Pony Express*. Helena, MT: Falcon, 1995.

Dolan, T. M. *Guns of the Pony Express*. New York: Linford, 1997.

Geis, Jacqueline. *The First Ride: Blazing the Trail for the Pony Express*. Nashville, Tenn.: Ideals, 1994.

Godfrey, Anthony. *Pony Express: Voyage of Discovery*. New York: KC Publications, 1999.

Gregory, Kristiana. *Jimmy Spoon and the Pony Express*. New York: Econo-Clad Books, 1999.

Hurwitz, Sue. *The Pony Express in American History*. Berkeley Heights, N.J.: Enslow, 2001.

Kroll, Steven. *Pony Express!* New York: Scholastic Press, 1996.

Johnston, Mairin. *The Pony Express*. New York: Attic Press, 1999.

McDonald, Brix. *Riding the Wind*. New York: Avenue Publications, 1998.

Moody, Ralph. *Riders of the Pony Express*. New York: Dell, 1990.

Yancey, Diane. *Life on the Pony Express*. San Diego: Lucent Books, 2001.

INTERNET RESOURCES

http://www.xphomestation.com/

http://www.americanwest.com/trails/pages/ponyexp1.htm

http://www.sfmuseum.org/hist1/pxpress.html

http://www.nps.gov/poex/

http://www.ponyexpress.org/

http://www.stjoseph.net/ponyexpress/

http://www.ci.st-joseph.mo.us/pony.html

http://www.usps.gov/history/his2.htm

http://www.ukans.edu/heritage/trails/pehist.html

http://www.utah.com/places/public_lands/pony_express.htm

http://www.ponyexpress.org/history.htm

INDEX

PHOTO CREDITS

ABOUT THE AUTHOR

John Riddle is a freelance writer and author with over 25 years' experience. His byline has appeared in the Washington Post, the New York Times, Delaware Today Magazine, and dozens of other publications. He is the author of six books, including *How to Start a Consulting Business* and *Managing Stress at Work*, and the co-author of *Family Health for Dummies* and *Men's Health for Dummies*. He has also written for over 100 websites, including Discovery Health.com, CBS Medscape.com, Office.com, and others. He is a frequent presenter and keynote speaker at many writers' conferences.